St. Louis Community College

Forest Park
Florissant Valley
Meramec

Instructional Resources
St. Louis, Missouri

SUPER-CHARGED!

ATV'S

BY

Paul Estrem

EDITED BY

Howard Schroeder, Ph.D.
Professor in Reading and Language Arts
Dept. of Curriculum and Instruction
Mankato State University

PUBLISHED BY

CRESTWOOD HOUSE

Mankato, MN, U.S.A.

CIP

LIBRARY OF CONGRESS CATALOGING IN PUBLICATION DATA

Estrem, Paul.
  ATV's.

  (Super-charged!)
  SUMMARY: Describes a variety of ATV's (all-terrain vehicles) and their uses. Includes
a glossary of terms.
  1. All terrain vehicles—Juvenile literature. [1. All terrain vehicles] I. Schroeder,
Howard. II. Title.
TL235.6.E88   1987   629.2'2042   87-19900
ISBN 0-89686-348-4

International Standard Book Number:	Library of Congress Catalog Card Number:
0-89686-348-4	87-19900

CREDITS

Illustrations:
Cover Photo: Specialty Vehicle Institute of America (SVIA)
SVIA: 5, 6, 13
Dick Young: 16-17
Don and Pat Valenti/Tom Stack & Associates: 18-19
Jim Yuskavitch/Tom Stack & Associates: 27
ATV News: 28, 42-43
Special thanks to *ATV Sports* magazine and photographers
Phil Beckman, Matt Hilgenberg, Dean Kirsten, and Bruce Simurda for the photos
on the following pages: 8, 11, 21, 22, 24-25, 31, 32-33, 34, 36-37, 38-39, 45
Graphic Design & Production:
Baker Street Productions, Ltd.
Technical Assistance:
Steven Jacobsen

CRESTWOOD HOUSE

Box 3427, Mankato, MN, U.S.A. 56002

TABLE OF CONTENTS

INTRODUCTION

Janet carefully placed the last piece of firewood on top of the pile in the trailer. She wiped her forehead with the back of her hand and stepped back to admire her work. The noon sun felt hot on her back.

Janet gazed at the meadow and forest surrounding her and smiled. She was glad that her aunt and uncle had invited her and her brother, Mike, to camp with them this week. Then Janet heard her aunt calling from the campsite down by the creek.

She cupped her hands around her mouth and faced the direction of the campsite. "I'm on my way, Aunt Jill!" she shouted as loudly as she could. She waited for an answer and heard a faint "We're ready to eat!" echo through the forest. Janet quickly put on her jacket and tossed her baseball cap into the trailer.

"Now for the fun part!" Janet cried as she walked around the trailer to Aunt Jill's "three-wheeler." She checked the trailer hitch, strapped on her helmet and hopped on. "Let's go, Baby Blue," Janet said as she turned the key. The machine roared to life. She glanced back to check the firewood in the trailer. Janet then slowly twisted Baby Blue's accelerator handle. They were off!

Janet drove quickly across the meadow in second gear. She shifted down to low gear when she approached the trees on the far side. She braked, turned the front

All-terrain vehicles can often turn work into fun!

wheel sharply, and slowly guided Baby Blue and the trailer between two large trees. She slowly twisted and turned past several more trees and then stopped.

Janet looked down a rolling, heavily wooded hill to the shallow creek below. She felt a shiver of excitement, but then remembered how easily Baby Blue had pulled her and the trailer up the hill. "Show me your brakes, Blue," Janet whispered as she shifted into low gear.

Even with a heavy load, this ATV can handle hills, streams and rough ground.

Janet eased Baby Blue and the trailer over the top of the hill. The three-wheeler's wide, knobby tires hugged the hill as Janet carefully braked and turned to keep the trailer upright. In less than a minute, they were at the bottom of the hill. And all the firewood was still in the trailer.

"You deserve a bath after that, Blue," Janet said as she gunned the engine. She shifted into low gear and the three-wheeler tugged the trailer across a flat, sandy bank into the shallow creek. Janet steered to the middle of the creek and started to drive slowly downstream. The sound of water lapping at the sides of the tires made

Janet want to speed up to make some spray. But then she remembered that Aunt Jill wouldn't be happy with wet firewood.

As Janet rounded a bend in the creek, she saw Aunt Jill and Mike standing by the campfire next to the creek. "I got a good load, Aunt Jill!" Janet shouted. In a few moments, she pulled up next to them in the creek and shut off the engine. "If you want some, you'll have to come out here to get it, though," she teased.

Aunt Jill smiled and opened her mouth to answer Janet's remark. Suddenly, they heard the sound of a loud, racing engine coming their direction from further downstream. Janet, Aunt Jill and Mike turned and saw Uncle Steve about a hundred yards (91 m) away from them. He was riding in the middle of the creek on Big Red, his trail bike. Water sprayed high above Uncle Steve on both sides as he pushed Big Red on the final stretch to the campsite.

As he drew close to Janet and Baby Blue, Uncle Steve gunned the engine, downshifted, and let the big trail bike slow itself to a stop. He shut off the engine, unsnapped his helmet and removed his goggles. "This looks like a pretty bored group of campers," Uncle Steve said, smiling. "Maybe I'm at the wrong campsite?"

"Let me take this trailer off, Uncle Steve, and it won't be boring," Janet replied. "Baby Blue's been itching to spin her wheels ever since I filled the trailer with firewood."

Honda's "Big Red" ATV makes camping even more of an adventure.

"Did you find Carl down by the lake?" Aunt Jill asked.

"I sure did," Uncle Steve answered. "And when we visit him after lunch, we'll get a chance to see some real ATV action, Janet. Carl has a machine that will leave both Big Red and Baby Blue behind. Let's get that firewood unloaded and have lunch. I'm starved!"

WHAT DOES "ATV" MEAN?

Right now, Janet is probably wondering what kind of an ATV her uncle's friend has. And you may be wondering what "ATV" means. The letters "ATV" are an abbreviation for "all-terrain vehicle." And what makes an all-terrain vehicle different from other vehicles?

First, an ATV is built to travel where other vehicles cannot go. Second, an ATV is built to provide power rather than speed. And third, an ATV is built to preserve the environment. Let's look at a few examples:

Two-Wheelers — A motocross motorcycle is built to run in high-speed races through mud, sand and gravel. In contrast, an ATV trail bike is built to haul heavy loads through the wilderness without cutting deep tracks in the ground.

Three-Wheelers and Four-Wheelers — Motorcycle

"trikes" and four-wheel go-karts are built to run on paved streets or tracks. A three- or four-wheel ATV, however, is built to travel easily over rough terrain.

Six-Wheelers — A speedboat is built to race across the water. A race car is built to run on a paved or dirt track. A six-wheel amphibian ATV can be driven through a forest, motored across a lake, and driven back into the forest again.

WHERE DID ATV'S COME FROM?

The first all-terrain vehicles were "work" vehicles used by telephone company linemen, construction workers, game wardens and ranchers in wilderness and mountain areas. They used the first ATV's to get to and from their jobs. Before ATV's, people usually had to ride horses or walk long distances. In fact, some areas were impossible to reach before ATV's were invented.

Hunters and fishermen also started to use ATV's to travel to their favorite remote hunting and fishing spots. Today, motorcycle and snowmobile manufacturers are offering a wide variety of ATV's to be used for fun. The new three- and four-wheelers are especially popular among younger people and their families. They are ideal for camping, exploring, trail riding and organized racing. Being able to ride rather than walk through wild,

Never say "never" with an ATV!

scenic areas has given many ATV riders a freedom they never had before.

WHO CAN DRIVE AN ATV?

You do not need a driver's license or special training classes to drive an ATV. (Special training and supervision for beginners is important, though.) Also, there are no age restrictions for ATV drivers. The reason? You cannot drive an all-terrain vehicle on public streets, roads or highways. ATV's are strictly "off-the-road" machines.

WHERE CAN YOU DRIVE AN ATV?

It is illegal and unsafe to drive an ATV of any kind on a public road. ATV's are not equipped with turn signals, rearview mirrors and other road-safety features. Most ATV's are too slow to keep up with automobile traffic.

ATV's can be driven only on private or government-approved property. Many states provide public ATV trails and "ditch-riding" rights similar to those allowed for snowmobiles. If you live in the country, it should be easy for you to find good places to ride. If you live in a city, you will have to find approved ATV trails or private property on which to ride.

12

Driving an ATV on snow or ice might not be a problem—but driving on any public road is. ATV's are strictly "off-the-road" vehicles.

MINIBIKES: THE "POCKET" SCOOTERS

Most motorized two-wheel vehicles are called "motorcycles" or "motorscooters." The "minibike" and "trail bike" are two exceptions. Both machines operate much the same as true cycles and scooters, but are legal for "off-road" ATV use only.

There are many types of minibikes. Most of them look like miniature versions of the larger trail bikes. A minibike usually comes with a small engine, light frame, and small, wide tires. Most of them weigh about fifty pounds (23 kg) and are easy for an adult to carry. Some minibikes can be broken down and folded up for easy storage.

You will often see minibikes attached to the backs of large campers and vans. Minibikes are also carried on board many large sailboats and cruisers. Outdoor researchers, service people, ranchers and sportsmen often carry minibikes in their cars or trucks.

What's the biggest value of a minibike? The answer is much the same as for other ATV's. Minibikes can be used when the only other choices are to walk or use a less convenient vehicle. People on vacation can quickly unpack and run errands on a minibike, rather than pulling their camper out of its site at a campground. Boaters can ride their minibikes from the dock to a store instead of walking. A rancher can tote a minibike in the back of his truck in case of an emergency. A fisherman can park his car in a parking lot and ride his minibike down a path to his favorite lake.

A basic minibike will often travel no faster than ten miles (16 km) per hour. The only controls are a simple rear-wheel brake and accelerator. A more expensive minibike may travel at speeds up to fifty miles (80 km) per hour. It also may have shock absorbers, disc brakes, lights, turn signals, and a multiple-speed transmission.

TRAIL BIKES:
THE BIG "MULES"

Like minibikes, off-road trail bikes are available in a variety of shapes and sizes. The main differences between them are power, ruggedness and weight. The minibike is designed to be easily carried. The trail bike is intended to provide the pulling power of a mule. In fact, the most powerful trail bikes can go places where other ATV's and mules or horses have to turn around.

What are the differences between trail bikes and other off-road motorcycles? First, the trail bike is designed to provide more power than speed. Its rugged transmission and powerful, reliable engine are geared to pulling and climbing rather than racing. It has a set of extra-low gears to provide the greatest amount of power possible.

Second, the trail bike is equipped with a rugged set of wide, oversized knobby tires. In fact, some trail bike tire treads look like the heavy treads on tractor tires. Third, the trail bike is supported and protected by a heavy-duty frame that will not bend or break under very hard use.

Who uses these tough-as-nails machines? Almost anyone who needs to get to places where other vehicles can't take them.

Minibikes and trail bikes are based on earlier off-road cycles, such as the MX cycle in this photo.

THREE-WHEEL ATV'S

Many of the first ''three-wheeler'' ATV's were designed for light pulling and hauling chores only. A small engine was most often used. It had low gear ranges. The machines were often enclosed in heavy, one-piece fiberglass bodies. The driver usually sat inside the machine, as in a golf cart.

In the past few years, motorcycle and snowmobile manufacturers have built more rugged models of the three-wheeler. These newer "trikes" have more motorcycle features than the earlier ones. For example, the driver now straddles the machine like a motorcycle. Motorcycle foot pegs are provided for the feet. The gearshift and brake levers are mounted on a set of motorcycle handlebars. And finally, the engine provides both

The driver of this ATV three-wheeler knows that a little snow never hurt anyone.

power and speed, similar to that of a motorcycle.

Three-wheelers are used for everything from hauling to exploring and racing. Because they are quite stable on the ground, they are ideal for hauling small trailers over rugged areas. They are also excellent for exploring, since their wide, knobby tires provide excellent traction. And because they have high-performance motorcycle engines, they provide thrilling excitement on a dirt track or hill climb.

THE NEW FOUR-WHEELERS

Similar to the newer "trikes," the new four-wheeler ATV's have many motorcycle features. The driver straddles the machine and places his feet on motorcycle foot pegs. The gearshift and brake levers are mounted on a set of motorcycle handlebars. The engine provides both power and speed, similar to that of a motorcycle.

One difference between the two types of vehicles is that the new four-wheelers are more stable than the "trikes," especially when cornering at higher speeds. The reason is that the front end is heavier and better balanced with two tires. A second important difference is that most four-wheelers are equipped with a reverse gear to help them turn around in tight quarters.

Like three-wheelers, these four-wheel machines are

Four-wheelers are more stable than the "trikes."

Like the three-wheelers, the four-wheeler can haul, race, and explore.

used for everything from hauling to exploring and racing. Selecting a three- or four-wheel machine is a matter of personal choice.

ODYSSEY RACERS

Odyssey racers aren't much bigger than the new three- and four-wheel ATV's. However, they look and perform quite differently. The driver sits close to the ground, as in a go-kart. Also, these racers are equipped with steering wheels rather than motorcycle handlebars. And the driver is protected by heavy-duty roll bars. Like other four-wheel ATV's, however, odyssey racers have small, wide tires and are equipped with powerful engines.

Odyssey events are extremely popular, and include several types of activities. Odyssey ice racing is held during the winter. Odyssey dirt-track racing and stunt driving are popular during the summer months. Spectators find these machines very entertaining because they're easy to flip over. Each race is full of spills, chills, rolls and tumbles!

Odyssey racers are four-wheel ATV's with a totally different look.

DUNE BUGGIES & BAJA BUGS

These modified cars are the ancestors of the new four-wheelers you can see in today's motorcycle showrooms. Dune buggies have been popular since the 1960's. They are still very popular today, especially in the southwestern and western states. All you need is a lot of sand and some big balloon tires!

Most dune buggies are modified Volkswagen "beetles." The owners usually make three main changes to their machines. First, they remove all the unnecessary parts and reinforce the frame. Second, they "beef up" the engine for more power. And finally, they remove the street tires and install large, wide "balloon" tires to give more traction in the sand. It's exciting to watch a dune buggy ramming toward the top of a sand dune, with sand flying in all directions and the engine roaring!

Baja bugs are built mainly for the Baja Run. This is a very hard endurance race in the Mexican desert. These machines look a lot like dune buggies, but have narrower tires and provide more protection for the driver. Spare parts and tires are usually strapped to the "bug" body, since the Baja is a very long run. If a part or tire fails, there's no service station for repairs!

The Baja Run is known as one of the world's hardest tests on a car's endurance. The driver's endurance is tested, too! Most of the cars in the Baja Run look funny

Dune buggies have been popular since the 1960's.

because of the way each driver prepares for the race. But if you look hard, you can see a good reason for everything that looks strange on a car. Water bags, spare parts, extra tires and tool kits are all there for a reason. The Baja is a tough run!

SWAMP BUGGIES

Swamp buggies are built for one reason: to get through the marshy swamps and bogs of Florida and Louisiana. Each swamp buggy looks different since each driver builds his or her own machine.

Baja bugs are similar to dune buggies, but are built especially for an endurance race in the Mexican desert.

Most swamp buggies have four wheels and a very powerful engine. Usually, at least two large tractor wheels are used. When the wheels spin fast enough, the buggy glides right over all the weeds and muck. But if the engine cuts out, the unlucky driver may get thrown out into the swamp from the high seat above the water!

SIX-WHEEL ATV'S

This all-terrain vehicle has a single-piece waterproof body. It can be driven in and out of the water without making any adjustments or getting the driver wet. Six-wheelers are equipped with six soft ''balloon'' tires that serve several purposes. The wheels leave practically no imprint or tracks on the terrain they cross. They hug the surface to provide maximum traction. And the wheels are ribbed to provide a ''paddling'' action in the water.

The six-wheel ATV is very popular with outdoor sportsmen, naturalists, game wardens and sightseers. It can be used as a fishing boat, duck blind, land cruiser or picnic wagon. The only drawback is that this little craft can be difficult to control in choppy waters. Some models are equipped with transoms on which to mount an outboard motor. Some of these machines can travel about 30 miles (48 km) per hour on land, and 5 miles (8 km) per hour in calm water.

Six-wheel ATV's come with a steering wheel, floor-mounted joysticks, or dash-mounted steering levers. Either floor pedals or joysticks can be used for throttling and braking. A reverse gear gives the driver a lot of freedom while moving around on land or in the water. Sometimes six-wheelers have top covers to protect passengers from the weather.

THE ATV RIDING "BASICS"

Whether or not you're new to ATV activities, you will enjoy riding most if you remember some riding and safety "basics." This is true no matter what kind of machine you are using. And the rules apply whether you're taking part in an organized event, digging around in the mud on a Saturday afternoon, or riding down a forest trail.

ATV's are built to take a lot of stress. But they have weaknesses, too. It's important to know what those weaknesses are. The ATV "basics" are important for another reason. You should understand them in order to protect yourself—and others—no matter where you're riding. Before you get ready to ride, you should always think about the following ATV "basics."

Knowing the ATV "basics" lets this driver enjoy his Yamaha Moto-4 100 ATV even more.

Clothing

Always wear proper clothing when you ride your machine. This is important for both comfort and safety. It's a good idea to think about what you're going to do on your machine before leaving.

Are you going to take your cousin for a quiet ride out by the barn? Your regular play clothes will be fine in good weather. But you will have to remember not to try anything fancy! Are you going to spend the morning exploring a wild off-the-road area with some friends on your three-wheeler? It would be smart to wear your most rugged protective gear. You may take a few spills.

Remember to keep all parts of your body completely

Whether competing or practicing, protective gear and proper clothing are always important.

covered while riding. This is always best for your safety. If you take a spill, you will have a better chance of not getting cuts and bruises. Shirts and jackets should be loose enough to let your arms move freely. Trousers or riding pants should be tight in the legs so they won't get caught in any moving parts.

What about shoes and socks? For most day-to-day casual riding, your favorite tennis shoes will be fine. For heavy racing or hill climbing, boots are the best choice. If you're wearing shoes, make sure they have laces and are tied securely. You won't want them to fall off during a tricky maneuver!

Frequent safety checks will help you spot any problems with your machine. You wouldn't want a breakdown in a situation like this!

Special Protective Gear

Selecting the right riding clothes is important. Using special protective gear is even more important. ATV riding can be a power-packed, rough-and-tumble sport. The best way to be prepared for a spill is to use proper gear at all times.

Head and face injuries can be very serious. Wearing a good helmet and goggles is the best way to avoid these injuries. Even if you're just going on a short, quiet trip, you should always wear your helmet.

Official competitions require that you wear special gloves, protective pads, boots and garments. Remember to wear them during practice, too!

You can find special riding pants, shirts, jackets and one-piece suits at most cycle shops. They are lightweight, rugged, and provide a lot of comfort and protection. Most of them have built-in protective pads.

Safety Check!

Before riding, you should always check over your machine. You can avoid many problems by using the simple ten-point checklist below. If you don't know how to adjust or fix a part, don't try to do it yourself!

1. Check handlebars or steering wheel for position and tightness. Check any protective gear on the machine.
2. Check front and rear brakes.
3. Check frame, body and suspension system.
4. Check wheel alignment and tightness.
5. Check wheel rim condition, tire condition and tire pressure.

These young drivers compare the Honda ATC110 and the Kawasaki KLT110.

6. Check condition and tightness of chain sprockets.
7. Check chain condition and tension.
8. Check engine and ignition system.
9. Check fuel supply.
10. Check all bolts and fasteners for tightness.

And don't forget: If you're going to park your machine, be sure that you use a strong safety chain and lock!

ATV Off-The-Road Rules

Whether you're racing, hill climbing or riding casually in a special ATV park, you should always keep the following set of riding rules in mind:

Never ride alone in a secluded area. Having other ATV fans around adds to the fun!

- Ask your local police department about ATV rules and respect the rules at all times.
- Never "ride" or "buck" a passenger on a one-passenger machine.
- Always yield to other vehicles and be polite to pedestrians. Use hand signals for stops and turns when you're riding.
- Always use extra caution at night or in bad weather.
- Always keep both hands on the handlebars or steering wheel.
- When riding in a secluded area, never ride alone!

AN ATV ADVENTURE

After a delicious lunch of fish, fried potatoes and wild berries, Janet helped Uncle Steve put out the campfire. Then Janet, Aunt Jill and Mike finished cleaning up the campsite as Uncle Steve wrapped and tied all their food in plastic bags. He hung the food from a rope high up in a tree to protect it from animals during the afternoon.

"There. I think we're ready to head for the lake," Uncle Steve said. "Janet, are you going to drive Baby Blue?"

"You bet I am!" Janet shouted as she turned and ran to the three-wheeler. "C'mon, you guys, let's get moving and see what Carl's up to down by the lake!"

All four campers then strapped on their helmets. Uncle Steve and Aunt Jill seated themselves on Big Red and Janet and Mike got on Baby Blue. Uncle Steve and Janet started the engines and shifted into low gear. They rolled the big trail bike and three-wheeler carefully into the creek and headed downstream.

The group rode slowly down the middle of the shallow creek. They rounded the first bend and entered a deep forest. The sun shone through the trees and made the water in the creek sparkle. Songbirds could be heard further down the creek. They rounded several more bends and then Uncle Steve signaled Janet to stop.

"Look—up there," Uncle Steve whispered. Everyone looked up a steep hill to where he was pointing.

They saw two deer looking at them with big eyes. The deer quickly turned and bounded over the top of the hill. Their white tails bobbed up and down as they ran.

"Wow," Mike whispered, "they were beautiful!" Aunt Jill turned and said, "We get to see wild animals all the time up here. Baby Blue and Big Red love to take us sightseeing. We may get to see those deer on the way back, too."

Soon, the creek straightened out and the woods became less dense. Janet thought she could see glimpses of the lake at the end of the creek. "Are we just about there, Uncle Steve?" Janet asked.

"Only a little way to go, Janet," Uncle Steve replied. "Is your sister driving okay, Mike?" Janet felt Mike poke her in the ribs as he said, "Not as well as a boy, but okay, I guess."

In a few minutes, the four riders drove up out of the creek onto the rocky lakeshore. Uncle Steve and Janet shut off the engines. Everyone climbed off, took off their helmets, and stretched. "That's Carl's cabin over there," Uncle Steve said, pointing at a log cabin a few hundred feet down the shore. "And that's Carl out there," he added, pointing at the lake.

Janet squinted at the lake and saw a small motorboat moving in their direction. The little boat was about fifty feet (15 m) from shore. "That's the silliest boat I've ever seen," Mike said. "It looks like a bug on the water."

The six-wheel ATV can go nearly everywhere—including the water.

"Do you think Carl will show us his new ATV when he gets here, Uncle Steve?" Janet asked. Uncle Steve laughed. "I'm sure he will," he replied.

"Uncle Steve, he's going to crash!" Janet cried suddenly. "He's not slowing down and he's heading

straight for the rocks!'' Janet looked at Uncle Steve and
was shocked to see him laughing. She heard Carl gun
the motor and turned back just in time to see Carl drive
the boat up out of the water and over the rocks. There
was no loud crash. And the boat had six tires that looked
like big, black beach balls! Carl drove his strange

machine over by his visitors and shut off the engine.

"Well, Janet, I told you Carl would probably show us his new ATV," Uncle Steve said. "And I also told you his machine would leave Big Red and Baby Blue behind. I don't think we could follow his new amphibian ATV back into the lake!"

IS ORGANIZED ATV RIDING FOR YOU?

Like Janet, maybe you're just getting your first taste of ATV riding. Or maybe you've been riding for a while but have never seen or taken part in an official ATV competition. How can you learn more?

The quickest way to learn more is to visit an ATV race or other event in your area. You will be able to meet lots of people who love ATV's and know a lot about them. They will be happy to tell you how to get involved.

Another way is to talk to your nearest ATV or motorcycle dealer. Dealers will be glad to tell you about ATV groups and events in your area. They can also tell you how to get ATV newsletters and magazines like *ATV Sports, ATV News,* and *Dirt Wheels.* This way, you can contact national ATV organizations and keep up with the latest developments in the world of ATV.

From Baja bugs to minibikes, swamp buggies to six-wheelers, the ATV world has plenty to offer you!

With ATV's, excitement is never far behind!

GLOSSARY / INDEX

ACCESSORIES 28, 32, 35 — *Extra or special equipment, such as helmets, gloves, and riding boots.*

AMPHIBIAN 10, 44 — *An all-terrain vehicle that can travel on both land and water.*

ATV 6, 8, 9, 10, 12, 14, 15, 16, 20, 23, 29, 30, 35, 38, 39, 40, 41, 44 — *Abbreviation for "all-terrain vehicle."*

BAJA 26, 28 — *A Mexican desert where a famous road race is held every year.*

CLOTHING 32, 33, 40

DOWNSHIFT 4, 7 — *To shift from a higher gear into a lower gear.*

DUNE BUGGY 26, 27, 28 — *A four-wheel ATV used to ride across sand.*

FOUR-WHEELER 9, 10, 20, 21, 22, 23, 26 — *A four-wheel all-terrain vehicle.*

GO-KART 10, 23 — *A small, motorized four-wheel racing car (not an ATV).*

JOYSTICK 30 — *A stick used for steering, connected to the floorboard of a vehicle or aircraft.*

MINIBIKE 13, 14, 15, 44 — *A compact, two-wheel motorized vehicle that weighs about 50 pounds (23 kg).*

GLOSSARY / INDEX